Geeky Girl

First published in 2004 by Conari Press,
an imprint of Red Wheel/Weiser, LLC
York Beach, ME
With offices at:
368 Congress Street
Boston, MA 02210
www.redwheelweiser.com

Acknowledgments on page 63

ISBN 1-57324-972-6

Typeset in Grumble, Freehand521, Signpainter-House Script, and Mrs. Eaves

Printed in Canada

FR

11 10 09 08 07 06 05 04
 8 7 6 5 4 3 2 1

The paper used in this publication meets the minimum requirements of the American National Standard for Information Sciences—Permanence of Paper for Printed Library Materials Z39.48-1992 (R1997).

A Geeky Litmus Test

1. How often does your VCR blink?
   a. After a power outage.
   b. Isn't it supposed to blink?
   c. Haven't you heard of DVDs?

2. Star Trek match-up.
See if you can match the actor with the character they played.

Uhura	Kate Mulgrew
Bones (McCoy)	Terry Farrell
Data	Geordi La Forge
LaVar Burton	DeForest Kelley
Captain Kathryn Janeway	Nichelle Nicholls
Jadzia Dax	Brent Spiner

3. The String Theory is
   a. what helped to aid in the invention of tampons.
   b. trying to prove the existence of parallel universes and extra spatial dimensions.
   c. a musical theory first conceived by Johann Sebastian Bach in 1710, explaining how sound is produced by various vibrating mediums.

4. THE BATTLE OF THE BULGE
   a. is a good reason to go on a diet.
   b. was a battle launched by Hitler to reduce Allied air power.
   c. is the reason for low-waist jeans.

5. THE LAST SHOES YOU BOUGHT:
   a. sling-back high heels.
   b. hiking boots.
   c. green high-top sneakers.
   d. furry Hobbit feet.

ANSWERS

1. 5 points for a. 10 for c. And zip for b.
2. Turn to page 62 for the correct matches.
   2 to 3 correct—10 points. 4 to 5 correct—15 points. 6 correct—20 points.
3. Ten points for b. Zilch for a and c.
4. Ten points for b. Zilch for a and c.
5. Zilch for heels. 10 points for b and c, and a whopping 50 for d.

From "Grand Geek" to "Maybe You're not Such a Geek After All!"

100.....................GRAND GEEK: You are a credit to the Geek race.
70-99...............There's Geek enough of you to go around.
50-69...............You need to hang out with some tried and true Geeks more
                       often; they're sure to rub off on you.
less than 50 .....Oh well, at least you'll learn something reading this book.

A geeky girl goes to the mall only to study group social dynamics.

Where Geeky DOES shop:

- ✓ Thrift stores
- ✓ Museum shops
- ✓ Food co-ops
- ✓ Amazon
- ✓ Flea markets
- ✓ Independent book stores
- ✓ EBay
- ✓ Used record stores

A geeky girl
read the book
AND saw
the movie.

American Splendor
Beloved
Lord of the Rings Trilogy
Snow Falling on Cedars
High Fidelity
Cry the Beloved Country
Breakfast at Tiffany's

Remains of the Day
Ghost World
Blade Runner
The Shipping News
Girl, Interrupted
The End of the Affair

Geeky Girl Chemistry

Blind Dates

A GOOD ONE:
They discuss the
big bang theory
over dinner and
practice it afterwards.

A BAD ONE:
She talks world politics.
He talks world wrestling.
Afterward, she splits
like an atom.

Dream Dates

Bill Gates

Max Fisher

Owen Wilson

Quentin Tarentino

Austin Powers

Frodo

Michael Moore

Camille Paglia

A geeky girl
does NOT
high-five.

A geeky girl does NOT refer to herself in the 3rd person.

A geeky girl does NOT do the wave.

A geeky girl does NOT play air guitar.

A geeky girl does NOT kiss hello.

A geeky girl does NOT need company to go to the bathroom.

A geeky girl does NOT participate in the electric slide.

A geeky girl does NOT go tanning.

North American Grizzly bear
aeolia american ursu

monarch butterfly
papilio rex regis

A geeky girl can appreciate the great outdoors.

century plant
agava parryi

goldfish
hippurus

spotted finch
interstinctus passer

In two languages.

snapping turtle
crepitus turtur

mountain laurel
mons montis laurea

A geeky girl knows how to pronounce

alveolate adj.: pitted like honeycomb.
Geeky Girl learned this word when she became an apiarist.

harassment n.: the act of annoying persistently.
Geeky knows where to put the emphasis.

intaglio n.: an ingraving or incised figure in stone or other hard material.
A word that stuck with Geeky from art history and came in handy on her most recent trip to Italy.

perspicacious adj.: having acute mental vision or discernment: See synonyms at SHREWD.
Geeky knows that geeky is as geeky knows...

prix fixe n.: a complete meal offered at a fixed price.
Geeky knows when the 'x' is silent.

redux adj.: brought back; returned.
used postpositively. *Geeky invented this word.*

You can't keep a geeky girl down.

Maria Mitchell (1818–1889)

In 1847, amateur astronomer Maria Mitchell scanned the night skies over Nantucket, spotted a comet, and promptly calculated its exact position. Unfortunately, the thirty-year-old librarian's discovery was not universally well-received: well-equipped male astronomers around the world were chagrined that they had been eclipsed by a woman with a tiny two-inch telescope.

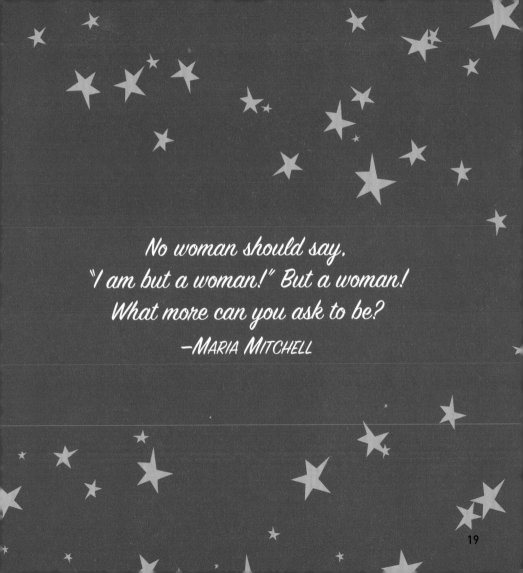

No woman should say,
"I am but a woman!" But a woman!
What more can you ask to be?
—MARIA MITCHELL

A geeky girl isn't worried about fitting in.
Unless she's on the subway.

A geeky girl is bilingual . . . she knows

A geeky girl knows:

- Her boyfriend's computer should be worth more than his car.
- How to use elisp.
- How to do an error-free installation of Windows XP, the first time.
- Only to boot DOS to play games.
- Not to send or receive mail that is not encrypted.

3.1415926

the difference between **UNIX** and **LINUX**

- If a program won't run under OSX then she obviously doesn't need it.
- The three laws of robotics and who invented them.
- The value of pi (to 10 digits).
- The difference between nuclear fission and fusion.
- Thinks the File/Kill command should apply to her boss.

A geeky girl

doesn't take vacations.
She has adventures.

☆ Wine-making in the Loire valley.

☆ Joining a dig for Mayan ruins in the rain forest.

☆ A literary walking tour of Prague.

☆ Exploring ancient Incan cities in Peru.

☆ Learning to skydive.

☆ Elephant-back safari in Chitwan National Park, Nepal.

A geeky girl is very label conscious.
About what she eats, not what she wears.

Organic Banana Chocolate Nut Smoothie

2	cups chocolate soy milk
2	large bananas
12	tablespoons high-protein soy powder
1/4	cup soy nut butter

Mix all ingredients in blender and purée until thick and smooth. Serve immediately or refrigerate. Makes about 4 cups.

A geeky girl
doesn't need
spell check.

conscience

hippopotamus

exuberant

incalescence

garrulous

kleptomaniac

non sequitur

pixilated

Five things
to keep a geeky girl
up all night.

① *System upgrade*

② Working her way through the kama sutra

③ A Dr. Who marathon

④ *The new Harry Potter Book*

⑤ Comet showers and a new high-powered telescope

All-Nighter Brownies

Melt 4 squares of bittersweet chocolate in a pan with 1 stick of butter. Set aside and let it cool. When it's room temp add:

2 scant cups of sugar
2 cups of flour
4 eggs
1 tsp of vanilla, or almond, or cherry extract

Bake for 30 minutes at 325°.

31

Athena is the geeky girl's goddess.

Athena was the goddess of wisdom and military victory, and also the patron of the city of Athens. She often helped heroes, like Jason and Perseus, and wore an aegis—a goatskin shield that had a fringe of snakes. When Perseus killed the gorgon Medusa, whose face turned men to stone, he gave the gorgon head to Athena, and the goddess placed it on her aegis.

FIG. 53. ATHENA

A geeky girl is self-propelled.

Geek Chic

Knows nada about Prada

Not trendy for Fendi

Glasses over Gucci

Books, not Balenciaga

Never seen in Alexander McQueen

Not showy in Chloé

*"I base most of my fashion taste
on what doesn't itch."* —GILDA RADNER

A geeky girl
exercises her mind
and her body.

Dear Geeky,

Dear Geeky,
Please help

Q. When do I program my new boyfriends into my cell?

Glam Girl

Dear Glam, Where else would you be keeping their numbers?

Q. I have a collection of love e-mails from my boyfriend. Is there any way I can keep them on my computer and make sure my boss can't read them?

Good Girl

Dear Good, You should never send or receive a personal e-mail that is not encrypted.

Q. My computer crashed a week ago and I haven't seen the Happy Mac since, should I be worried?

Grumpy Girl

Dear Grumpy, Have you seen the sad Mac? If so, be very, very sad.

Q. I'm falling for a guy who loves Monday night football. Is there any hope for this relationship?

a sister Geek

Dear Sister, If he'll switch to PBS at half-time, there's hope.

A geeky girl is not searching the universe for more intelligent life forms. She's already found one.

"Cats, as a class, have never completely got over the snootiness caused by the fact that in Ancient Egypt they were worshiped as gods. This makes them prone to set themselves up as critics and censors of the frail and erring human beings whose lot they share."
—P.G. WODEHOUSE

Confucius, Chinese philosopher extraordinaire, believed his cat was sent to him from the heavens to impart inspired wisdom. Cats are good for that, you know.

"The trouble with sharing one's bed with cats is that they'd rather sleep on you than beside you."
—PAM BROWN

Behind every great

"I suppose I could have stayed at home
and baked cookies and had teas."
—HILLARY RODHAM CLINTON, WIFE OF THE FORTY-SECOND
PRESIDENT OF THE UNITED STATES OF AMERICA

"Every politician should have been born
an orphan and remain a bachelor."
—LADY BIRD JOHNSON, WIFE OF THE THIRTY-SIXTH
PRESIDENT OF THE UNITED STATES OF AMERICA

man is a geeky girl.

"Well, I've got you the presidency,
what are you going to do with it?
—Florence Harding, wife of the twenty-ninth
president of the United States of America

"Behind every successful man
is a surprised woman."
—Maryon Pearson,
former Canadian Prime Minister's wife

A Lesson
in Geek History

Age Two

Halloween, Age 8

Kennedy High School

Grade 10

Subject	Qtr. 1	Qtr. 2	Qtr. 3	Qtr. 4
Honors English	A	A	A	A
Advanced Algebra	A	A	A	A
Physics	A	A	A	A
Latin	A	A	A	A
Phys. Ed.	D	D	D	D
Art	A	A	A	A
World Cultures	A	A	A	A

Junior prom

Ritz Theatres
ADMIT ONE
ROCKY HORROR
PICTURE SHOW

Comments: *Geeky is a joy to have in class. I recommend that she skip eleventh grade.*

"Certainly knitting is not the only thing that fingers can do, but it is a good thing: simple yet capable of endless complexity."
—From *Knitting for Anarchists*, Anna Zilboorg, 2002

"Although she continued to knit, and sat upright, it was thus that she felt herself; and this self having shed its attachments was free for the strangest adventures."
—From *To the Lighthouse*, Virginia Woolf, 1927

Scarf Pattern:

Using size 10 needles and 50-gram balls of yarn, cast on 20 stitches. Knit every row for 10 rows. Then knit a row and purl a row until you are within ten inches of the desired length. Using the grid here, on knit rows, purl pattern stitches and on purl rows knit pattern stitches. Repeat for a geeky girl monogram. To finish scarf, knit garter stitch for ten rows. Bind off when length is reached.

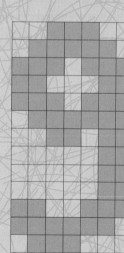

When it comes to friends
it's quality, not quantity.

"Each friend represents a world in us, a world possibly not born until they arrive, and it is only by this meeting that a new world is born."
—ANAIS NIN (1937),
THE DIARY OF ANAIS NIN

"I now know all the people worth knowing in America and I find no intellect comparable to my own."
—MARGARET FULLER

Geeky can also be her own best friend. "I paint self-portraits because I am so often alone, because I am the person I know best."
—FRIDA KAHLO

There's no reason to suffer fools gladly." Any girl can be glamorous. All you have to do is stand still and look stupid."
—HEDY LAMARR

A geeky girl knows the difference between a porter and a lager.

"Give me a women who truly loves beer, and I will conquer the world." –KAISER WILHELM THE SECOND

Beer has been made since 6000 B.C. (although it did go out of vogue for a while because the ancient Greeks thought it caused leprosy), and women made and sold most of it.

A geeky girl reads between the lines.

Virginia Woolf wrote all of her novels standing up.

One of the best-loved novels of all time, *Little Women* was written solely for the money. **Louisa May Alcott** hated young girls but was desperate for cash.

The reclusive **Emily Dickinson** wrote nearly 1,000 poems in her lifetime, but only 4 of them were published when she was alive.

The best-selling novel of the 1800's was *Uncle Tom's Cabin* by Harriet Beecher Stowe. Abraham Lincoln claimed it to be the impetus for the Civil War, saying of Stowe, "Is this the little lady whose book made such a war?"

The best-selling novelist of all time is Agatha Christie. Her 78 mysteries have sold more than 2 billion copies. It so happens that Christie was married to an archaeologist. When asked how that was, she replied, "It's wonderful. The older I get, the better he likes me."

There is no frigate like a book to take us lands away.

—EMILY DICKINSON

A geeky girl knows the meaning and proper usage of:

CV → *Curriculum Vitae* (Curricula Vitae when you're talking about more than one person.)

e.g. → *for example*

RSVP → *respondez s'il vous plait* (Never use the French with the English—as in Please respondez s'il vous plait by December 10th.)

Per se → by, of, or in itself or oneself or themselves as such : intrinsically.

N.B. → *nota bene* (a Latin phrase (or its abbreviation) used to indicate that special attention should be paid to something)

AD → *anno domini*

BC → *before Christian era*

cv

BC

e.g.

AD

N.B.

Per se

RSVP

Geeky Guiding Lights

Meg Whitman,
President & CEO,
eBay Technologies

Probably one of the
richest woman CEOs in
America, thanks to her eBay
stock options and the company's
outstanding IPO. Ranked third on
Fortune's Most Powerful Women list, Whitman
is steadily guiding one of the very few dot-com
companies in making money.

Carleton "Carly" Fiorina,
President & CEO,
Hewlett-Packard Company

A former AT&T employee, Fiorina was named the most powerful woman in American business by Fortune magazine before joining HP. She had successfully guided a spinoff company, Lucent Technologies Inc., out from the shadow of AT&T and through an IPO worth $3 billion.

Geeky girls give thanks...

TO GILDA RADNER, who was far more than just funny, for saying, "While we have the gift of life, it seems to me that the only tragedy is to allow part of us to die—whether it is our spirit, our creativity, or our glorious uniqueness."

TO HILLARY CLINTON, former first lady and current Senator, for saying, "There cannot be true democracy unless women's voices are heard. There cannot be true democracy unless women are given the opportunity to take responsibility for their own lives."

TO AMELIA EARHEART, the first woman to fly the Atlantic, for saying, "Women must try to do things as men have tried. When they fail their failure must be but a challenge to others."

TO KATHARINE HEPBURN, who always wore the pants in her household, for saying, "Life is to be lived. If you have to support yourself, you had bloody well better find some way that is going to be interesting. And you don't do that by sitting around wondering about yourself."

TO BJORK, one of the more unusual vocalists in all of popular music, for saying, "All people have their own way of dealing with everyday problems. Some go for walks, others get drunk, and some get laid. I write songs."

Key for Star Trek match-up!

Uhura . . . . .Nichelle Nicholls
Bones (McCoy) . . . . .DeForest Kelley
Data . . . . .Brent Spiner
LaVar Burton . . . . .Geordi La Forge
Captain Kathryn Janeway . . . . . . .Kate Mulgrew
Jadzia Dax . . . . .Terry Farrell

Acknowledgments

Grateful acknowledgment is made to the following for permission to reprint material copyrighted by them:

Alicia Alvrez, *The Ladies Room Reader*, © 2000 by Conari Press. On pages 53, 54

Erin Barrett and Jack Mingo, *Cats Don't Always Land on Their Feet*, © 2002 by Erin Barrett and Jack Mingo. Reprinted by permission of Red Wheel/Weiser. On page 42

Ame Mahler Beanland and Emily Miles Terry, *It's a Chick Thing*, © 2000 by Ame Mahler Beanland and Emily Miles Terry. Reprinted by Permission of Red Wheel/Weiser. On page 36

Autumn Stephens, *Wild Women: Crusaders, Curmudgeons, and Completely Corsetless Ladies in the Otherwise Virtuous Victorian Era*, © 1992 by Autumn Stephens. Reprinted by permission of Red Wheel/Weiser. On pages 18, 19

Autumn Stephens, *Wild Words from Wild Women*, © 1993 by Autumn Stephens. Reprinted by permission of Red Wheel/Weiser. On pages 44, 45, 51